101 Cute VALENTINE'S DAY Jokes

What kind of dinner does
Cupid eat?

A heart-y one.

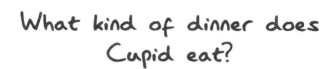

What do olives say to each
other on Valentine's Day?

Olive you.

Why do melons have to get
married in churches?

Because they cantaloupe!

3

What did one pig say to
the other?

Don't go bacon my heart.

Why do skunks love
Valentine's Day?

Because they're
scent-imental animals!

If you were a triangle,
you'd be acute one.

4

Did you hear about the two radios that got married?

The reception was amazing.

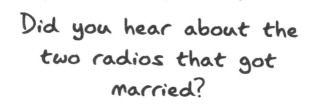

What did one snake say to the other on Valentine's Day?

Give me a hug and a hiss, honey.

Are you a loan? Because you definitely have my interest.

5

What's a bread loaf's favorite song?

"All You Knead is Love."

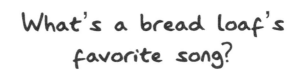

Why is getting your partner a kitten for Valentine's Day a good idea?

It's the purr-fect gift.

Did you hear about the vampire wedding?

It was love at first bite.

Did you hear about the spider wedding?

Yes, they're newly-webs.

Roses are red, violets are blue: I sure am glad I swiped right on you.

"I love bee-ing with you, honey" said one bee to the other on Valentine's Day.

What do you call two birds
in love?

Tweethearts

Is your name Google?

Because you have everything
I'm searching for.

Artichokes are the most
loving of vegetables: they
have hearts.

8

What's it called when two boats fall in love?

A row-mance.

Do you have a date for Valentine's Day?

Yes, February 14th.

I don't have a library card, but do you mind if I check you out?

What do farmers give their wives on Valentine's Day?

Hogs and kisses!

Do you know what you'd look really beautiful in this Valentine's Day?

My arms.

You look like you're suffering from a lack of vitamin me.

10

Did you hear about the bed bugs who fell in love?

They're getting married in the spring!

What did one light bulb say to his sweetheart on Valentine's Day?

I love you a whole watt.

What is the fish's valentine?

His Gil-Friend

What did one pickle say to the other?

You mean a great dill to me.

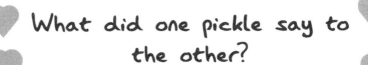

Today I got 150 Valentines cards, I was totally shocked and breathless

The security guard at Hallmark nearly caught me!

Why are artichokes so beloved?

They're known for their hearts.

What did the painter say
to her boyfriend?

I love you with all my art!

Knock, knock.

Who's there?

Emma.

Emma who?

Emma hoping I get lots of
cards on Valentine's Day!

Are you a parking ticket?

Because you've got fine
written all over you.

How did the phone propose
to his girlfriend?

He gave her a ring.

What did one cantaloupe
write to the other in their
Valentine's card?

"You're one in a melon!"

What grade did St.
Valentine get on his exam?

Be Mine(us).

Why shouldn't you fall in love with a pastry chef?

They'll dessert you.

Knock, knock.

Who's there?

Peas.

Peas who?

Peas be my Valentine!

What did the boy cat say to the girl cat on Valentine's Day?

You're purr-fect for me!

What did the bat say to their Valentine?

You're fun to hang around with.

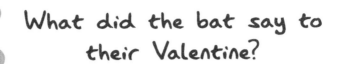

Did you hear about the person who used to open hundereds of cards on Valentine's Day?

Eventually, the post office fired him for it.

What do you call someone who was born on Valentine's Day?

A love child.

What did the love-obsessed candle say when it was lit?

"I found the perfect match!"

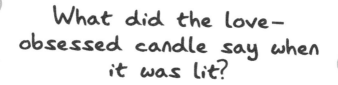

Knock, knock.

Who's there?

Luke.

Luke who?

Luke who got a Valentine!

What did one rabbit say to the other on Valentine's Day?

Some bunny loves you!

What did one piece of
toast say to the other on
Valentine's Day?

You're my butter half.

What do you call a ghost's
true love?

Their ghoul-friend.

Why did the magnet hit on
the refrigerator?

He found her to be very
attractive.

18

What kind of flower should you never give on Valentine's Day?

A cauliflower!

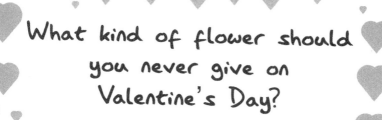

Why don't you ever date a tennis player?

Because love means nothing to them!

What do you call someone with a cold on Valentine's Day?

"Lovesick."

What happened to the two angels who got married?

They lived harpily ever after.

Why did the orange ask the banana to be their Valentine?

It was very a-peel-ing.

What type of flowers do sailors give on Valentine's Day?

Forget-me-knots.

What did the one sheep
say to the other?

I love ewe!

And how did the other
sheep answer?

You're not so baaaaaa-d
yourself.

Why didn't the two dogs
make serious Valentine's Day
plans?

It was just puppy love.

21

What did the squirrel tell
the other squirrel on
Valentine's Day?

I'm nuts about you!

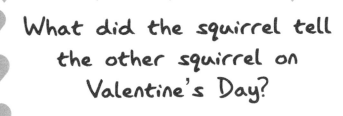

Why is Valentine's Day a
good day for a party?

Because you can really
party hearty!

What did the chocolate
sauce say to the ice cream?

I'm sweet on you.

22

Why did the police officer
lock up her Valentine?

For stealing her heart.

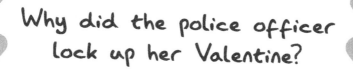

Why did the girl's family
approve of her dating a
goalie?

They thought he was a real
keeper!

What is the most romantic
of all ships?

A Court-ship.

Which flowers do squirrels
give each other on
Valentine's Day?

Forget-me-nuts.

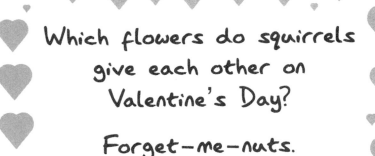

How did the pickleball flirt
with the paddle?

He said, "Hit me up
anytime!"

What did one bike say to
the other bike?

I wheelie like you.

Do you believe in love at first sight, or should I walk by again?

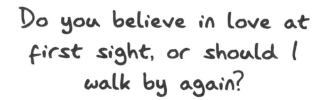

I'm sorry, I need to take you to jail.

You just stole my heart.

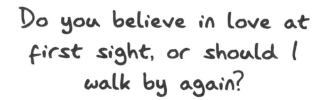

What can get you in trouble with the law on Valentine's Day?

Stealing too many hearts.

What did the light bulb
say to the switch?

You turn me on.

There's something wrong
with my cell phone. It
doesn't have your number in
it.

How did the two prunes
confirm dinner plans?

They said it was a date.

26

What did the caveman give his girlfriend on Valentine's Day?

Ughs and kisses!

Knock, knock.

Who's there?

Sherwood.

Sherwood who?

Sherwood like to be your Valentine!

What did the acrobat do on Valentine's Day?

He fell head over heels

What did the pasta say to the tomato?

I love it when you get saucy.

Knock, knock.
Who's there?
Jimmy.
Uh, Jimmy who?
Jimmy a little kiss.

How do you tell if a calendar is popular?

It has lots of dates.

The janitor told his wife on Valentine's Day?

You sweep me off my feet.

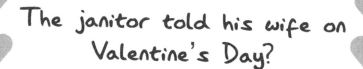

Did you hear what the map said to the compass?

I'm lost without you.

What did the guy with a sprained ankle tell his nurse?

I've got a crutch on you.

What did the Valentine's Day card say to the stamp?

Stick with me and you'll go places!

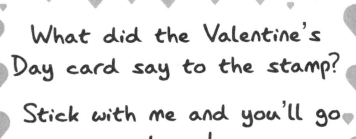

What did the bird say to the other bird while on Valentine's Day?

You're just ducky.

Which type of flower is the best at giving smooches?

Tulips.

On Valentine's Day the raisin said to the apple, how about a date?

"I like you a bot. In fact, I'm nuts and bolts about you" said the robot.

One lemon told another lemon...

you're my main squeeze.

What did the elephant say
to his sweetheart on
Valentine's Day?

I love you a ton.

Knock knock.

Who's there?

Howard.

Yes, Howard who?

Howard you'd like to be my
Valentine?

What did one citrus fruit
say to the other citrus
fruit?

Will you be my Valen-lime?

What did one scientist say
to the other?

We've got great chemistry.

What do you call an
affectionate dog on
Valentine's Day?

A Smooch Pooch.

The carpet salesman gave
his wife rugs and kisses
for Valentine's Day.

What did one piece of
toast say to the other?

You're my butter half.

The butter told the bun
that just came out of the
oven on Valentine's Day...

You're hot!

You can count on me said
the calculator to the pencil
on Valentine's Day.

What did one lamp say to the other?

You light up my life.

What did one drum say to the other drum on Valentine's Day?

My heart beats for you.

What did the bread say to the knife on Valentine's Day?

You look sharp.

What did one canoe say to another canoe?

You rock my boat.

Do you have a date for Valentine's Day?

I do. It's February 14.

xoxo

Printed in Great Britain
by Amazon

17773564R00031